BOOK 2

ROMANTIC IMPRESSIONS

MARTHA MIER

Romantic Impressions was especially written to provide pianists with the experience of expressive playing. Playing in a lyrical, expressive and romantic style is an important aspect in the development of the intermediate pianist.

Warm, lyrical, cantabile melodies and rich harmonic structures are found in this collection, which will appeal to pianists of any age who harbor a romantic soul!

It is my wish that playing this music will bring out the romantic in you, and leave you with lasting Romantic Impressions!

Martha Mier

CONTENTS

At a Sidewalk Cafe 10

Dreams Bright and Beautiful 5

Frosted Windowpanes 15

Glowing Embers 18

Nocturne 8

October Morning 2

Song of Seville 12

Starlight 21

Alfred Music
P.O. Box 10003
Van Nuys, CA 91410-0003
alfred.com

ISBN-10: 0-7390-0908-7
ISBN-13: 978-0-7390-0908-6

Cover Art:
The Artist's Garden at Giverny (1900) by Claude Monet (French, 1840-1926)
Musée d'Orsay, Paris; courtesy Giraudon/Art Resource, New York

for Dorothy Colvin

OCTOBER MORNING

Martha Mier

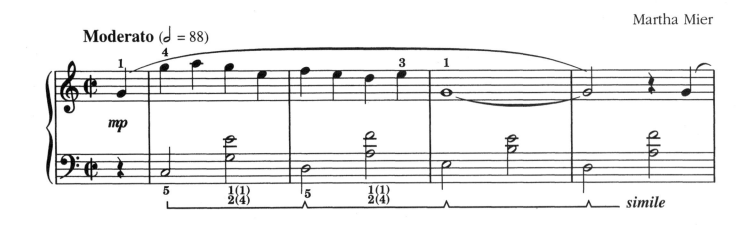

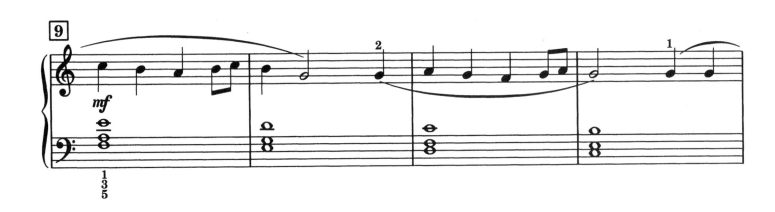

DREAMS BRIGHT AND BEAUTIFUL

Martha Mier

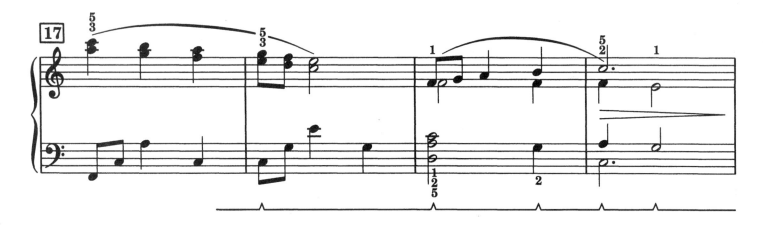

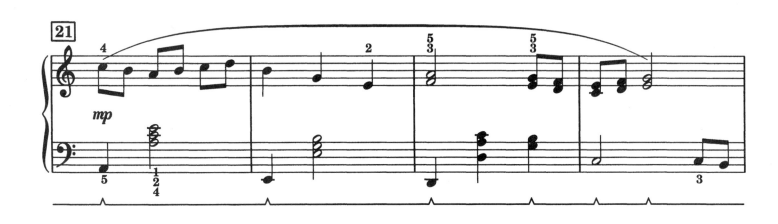

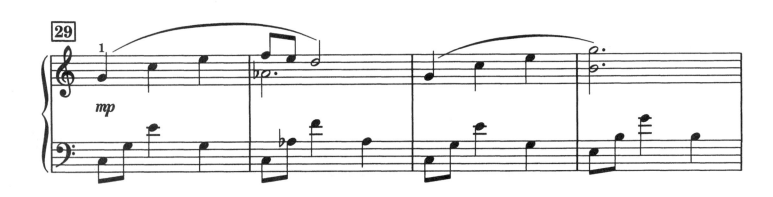

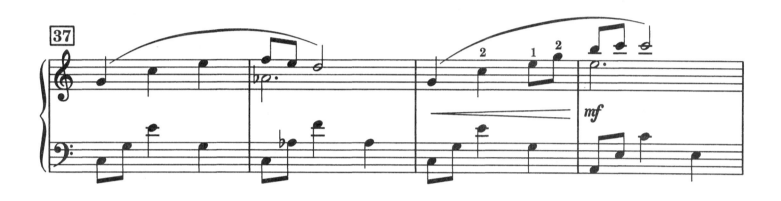

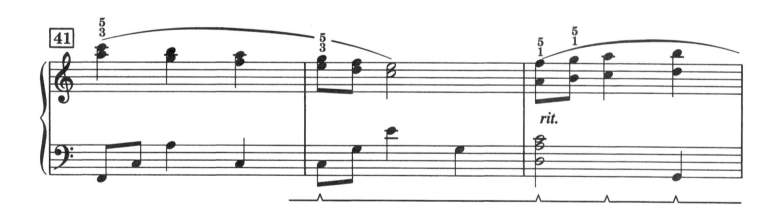

NOCTURNE

Martha Mier

Andante cantabile, con rubato

for Marcia Kazmierski

AT A SIDEWALK CAFE

Martha Mier

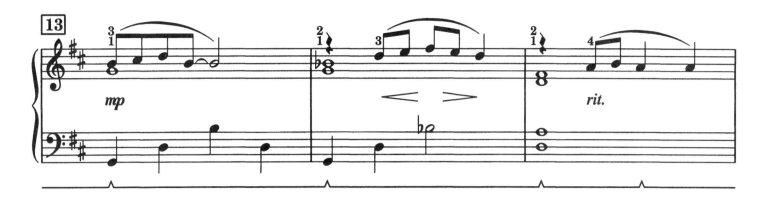

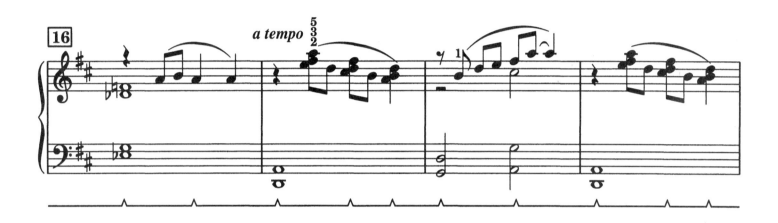

for Thomas Alan Mier

SONG OF SEVILLE

Martha Mier

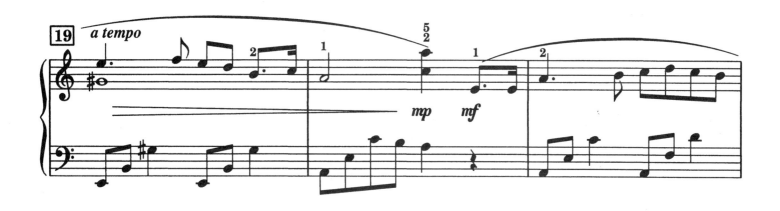

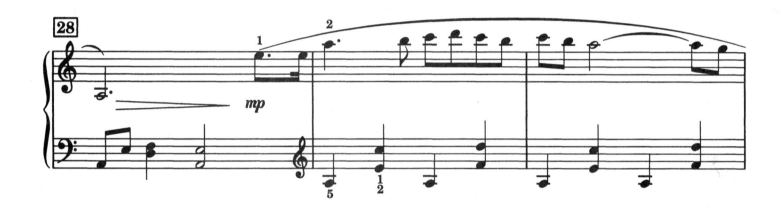

FROSTED WINDOWPANES

Martha Mier

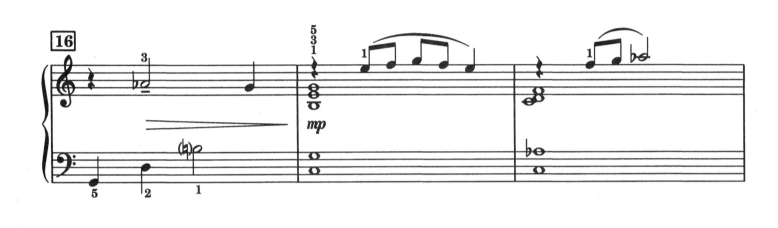

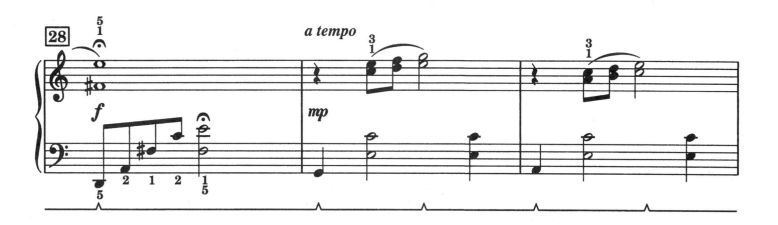

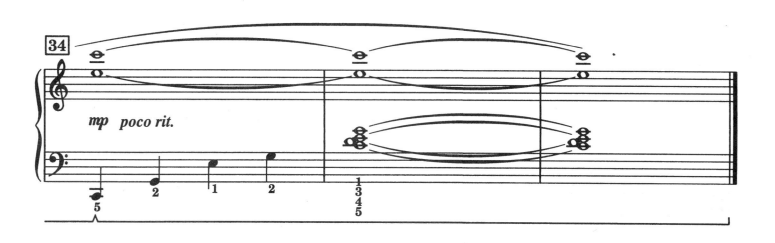

GLOWING EMBERS

Martha Mier

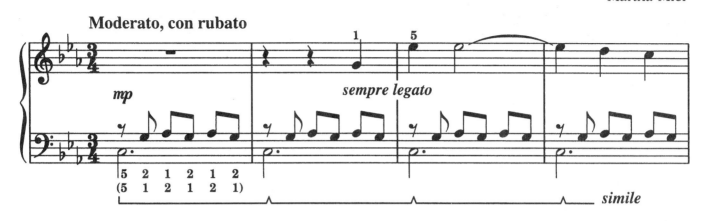

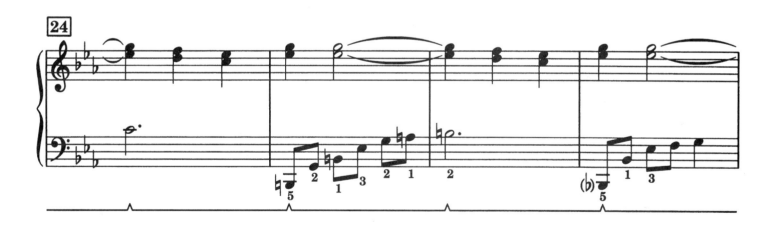

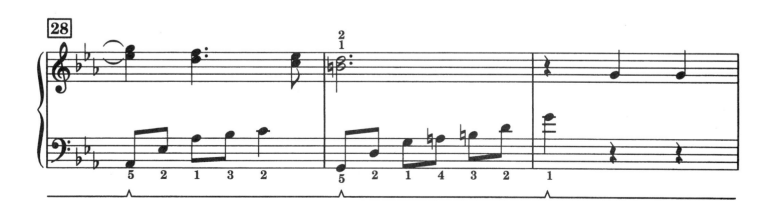

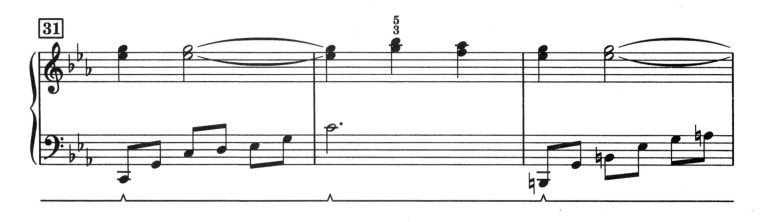

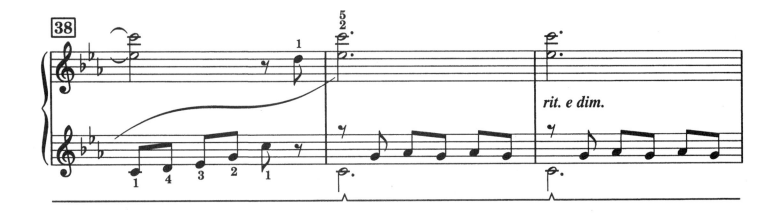

STARLIGHT

Martha Mier

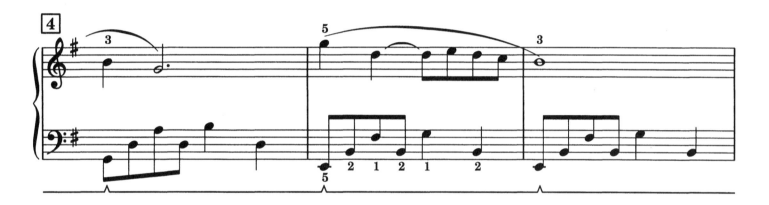

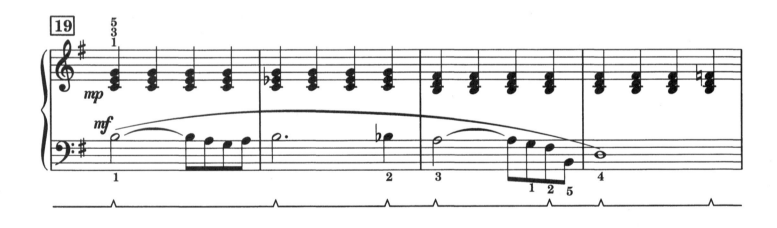

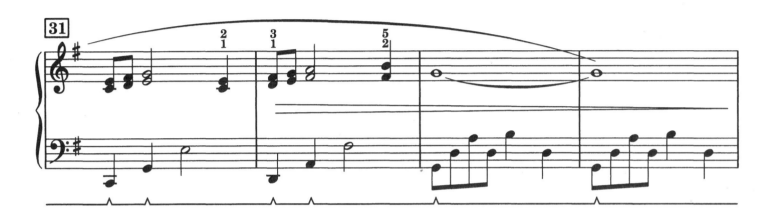